DOMINOES

D0667714

A Close Shave™

LEVEL TWO   700 HEADWORDS

OXFORD
UNIVERSITY PRESS

Great Clarendon Street, Oxford OX2 6DP

Oxford University Press is a department of the University of Oxford.
It furthers the University's objective of excellence in research, scholarship,
and education by publishing worldwide in

Oxford New York

Auckland Cape Town Dar es Salaam Hong Kong Karachi
Kuala Lumpur Madrid Melbourne Mexico City Nairobi
New Delhi Shanghai Taipei Toronto

With offices in

Argentina Austria Brazil Chile Czech Republic France Greece
Guatemala Hungary Italy Japan Poland Portugal Singapore
South Korea Switzerland Thailand Turkey Ukraine Vietnam

OXFORD and OXFORD ENGLISH are registered trade marks of
Oxford University Press in the UK and in certain other countries

This edition © Oxford University Press 2010

The moral rights of the author have been asserted

Database right Oxford University Press (maker)

First published in Dominoes 2007

2014 2013 2012 2011 2010

10 9 8 7 6 5 4 3 2

ISBN: 978 0 19 424881 5 BOOK
ISBN: 978 0 19 424833 4 BOOK AND MULTIROM PACK
MULTIROM NOT AVAILABLE SEPARATELY

No unauthorized photocopying

Printed in China

This book is printed on paper from certified and well-managed sources.

ACKNOWLEDGEMENTS

Illustrations by: Robin Edmonds pp 6, 7, 12, 18, 31, 39, 46, 54

The publisher would like to thank the following for permission to reproduce photographs: Corbis pp58
(Alexander Graham Bell, 1876), 60 (Mobile phone/W. Geiersperger), 60 (Apple Video iPod/
ZUMA/Krista Kennell/), 60 (Teens playing computer games/Darama), 60 (Skateboarding/
Reuters/Mike Blake); OUP p 60 (Internet address of a website over keys/imageshop);
Science and Society Picture Library pp 58 (Karl Friedrich Benz c.1900), 58 (Electric filament
lamps 1878-1879), 58 (Benz 1.5 hp motor car, 1888), 58 (Broadcast receiver, c 1925), 58
(Marconi phone television receiver, model 707, c 1938); Science Photo Library pp58 (John
Logie Baird), 58 (Guglielmo Marconi/Humanities & Social Sciences Library/NY Public
Library), 58 (Thomas Edison/Humanities & Social Sciences Library/NY Public Library), 58
(The Wright brothers/Humanities & Social Sciences Library/NY Public Library), 58 (Early
telephone constructed by Alexander Bell/J.L. Charmet), 58 (Wright flyer/US Air Force), 60
(Communications satellite/GE Astro Space).

DOMINOES

Series Editors: Bill Bowler and Sue Parminter

A Close Shave™

Based on Nick Park's
Oscar®-Winning Characters

Text adaptation by Bill Bowler

The Dominoes edition of *A Close Shave* is based on Nick Park's Oscar®-Winning Characters. Nick Park is a three-time Academy Award® Winner in the category of Best Animated Short for the films *Creature Comforts*, *The Wrong Trousers* and *A Close Shave*. All three films were created at Aardman, where Nick is a Co-Director with founders Peter Lord and David Sproxton. At Aardman, Nick has also served as a director and animator on numerous projects including pop promos, title sequences, and inserts for children's television. Another Wallace and Gromit story, *The Wrong Trousers*, is also available in the Dominoes series.

OXFORD
UNIVERSITY PRESS

BEFORE READING

1 Look at the diagram and answer the questions about the characters in *Wallace and Gromit: A Close Shave*.

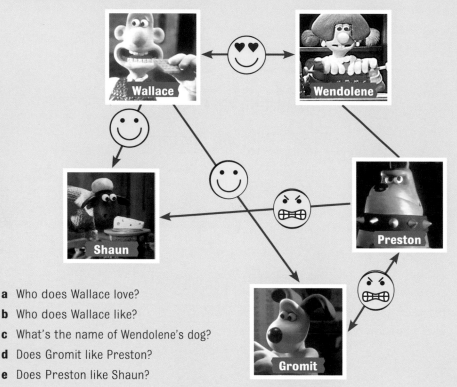

a Who does Wallace love?

b Who does Wallace like?

c What's the name of Wendolene's dog?

d Does Gromit like Preston?

e Does Preston like Shaun?

2 What do you think happens? Choose the words to complete sentences about the story.

a Wallace's new machine works well goes wrong.

b Wendolene sells sweets wool in her shop.

c Shaun comes to live with Wallace Wendolene.

d Gromit Shaun always helps Wallace with his machines.

e Shaun Preston helps everyone when they are in trouble.

f Wallace and Wendolene get married don't get married in the end.

Chapter 1

A visitor in the night

It was two o'clock in the morning, the sky was dark, and everything was quiet in West Wallaby Street. At number 62, Wallace was asleep in bed. There was a plate of **cheese** on the cupboard next to his bed. Cheese was Wallace's favourite food. Suddenly the room shook, and the cheese knife fell off the plate to the floor, but Wallace didn't wake up. His dog, Gromit, was in the next room, but he wasn't asleep. He was sitting up in bed, and he was **knitting**. His room started shaking too, and he heard a noise in the street. What was making the noise? Why was the house shaking? Gromit wasn't interested. He just went on knitting.

A big green **lorry** was driving past in front of the house, and it stopped at a red traffic light. The lorry was full of sheep, and when it stopped, a small sheep escaped from the back of the lorry. It jumped into the street, and ran away. The passenger who was sitting next to the lorry driver wanted to get out and catch the small sheep, but the driver stopped him. So the passenger stayed in his seat, but he looked out of the window and watched the sheep carefully. It was hurrying down the garden of number 62 West Wallaby Street. The passenger looked carefully at the house and read the **sign** on the wall.

cheese yellow food that you make from milk

knit to make clothes from wool using two small sticks

lorry a kind of big car for carrying things

sign writing in a place that tells people about something important

clean to stop something being dirty

> Wallace and Gromit's
> Wash and Go Window **Cleaning**

Then the traffic lights changed to green, and the big lorry drove away.

Upstairs at number 62, Gromit finished his last ball of **wool** and went to sleep. The small sheep pushed through a small door at the back of the house, but Gromit didn't hear anything.

Later that morning, Gromit was sitting in the kitchen. He was enjoying a quiet cup of tea and reading the newspaper. The **headline** on the front page of the newspaper said:

NO WOOL IN THE SHOPS!

Suddenly there was a noise from a **machine** in the corner of the kitchen. It was Wallace's special *Getting-Up-In-the-Morning* machine and the *Breakfast* light was going on and off. Upstairs Wallace was still in bed. He called lazily downstairs to Gromit, 'It's **porridge** for breakfast today, Gromit. It's Tuesday.'

Gromit pulled the **lever** of the *Getting-Up-In-the-Morning* machine. The head of Wallace's bed went up, and Wallace moved quickly down to the bottom of his bed, went through a door in the floor of the bedroom, and fell into the room below it. On the way, he fell into his trousers, and then onto a chair at the kitchen table. The machine quickly put a white shirt on Wallace, and he was ready for breakfast. He picked up a spoon from the table in front of him, and Gromit hit a red **button** on the *Porridge Machine*. A plate jumped out of the table in front of Wallace, and a gun started to shoot porridge into it.

But this Tuesday morning something went wrong. The gun began shooting porridge at Wallace and not into the plate. At first Wallace held his plate up to catch the porridge, and then, when the plate was full, he put his hands in front of his face to stop the porridge, but again and again the gun shot porridge at him.

wool the hair of a sheep; we use it to make warm clothes

headline the biggest words in a newspaper

machine something that does work for people

porridge a hot cereal that people eat for breakfast in England and specially Scotland

lever a long thing that you move to make a machine work

button a small round thing that you push to make a machine work

'Ow! Ow!' said Wallace. 'Turn it off, Gromit!' he cried.

Gromit walked to the *Porridge Machine* and hit another button to turn it off.

'Ooof,' said Wallace. He now had porridge all over his face, in his eyes, in his ears, and all over his shirt, and there was porridge all over the wall behind him, too.

Gromit looked at the black **wire** that went from the wall into the *Porridge Machine*. It was nearly in two pieces, and Gromit could see smaller red, yellow, and blue wires inside it. 'Something's eaten this,' he thought when he saw the wires.

'Do we have mice in the house?' Wallace asked, while he cleaned the porridge off his face.

Gromit looked behind him. Was there something there? Something strange was happening. He decided to look around the house to see what it was.

'I think that I'll make my porridge myself,' said Wallace, and he walked over to look in the food cupboard.

Gromit stopped in the **hall** next to a **plant**. There was a big hole in one of its leaves. 'Something's eaten that, too,' he thought.

wire a long, very thin, metal thing in a machine

hall a room in the middle of a house from which you can go to all the other rooms

plant a small green thing, with leaves, and sometimes with flowers

3

Wallace went to the kitchen cupboard, and took out the box of porridge. But there was a big hole in the bottom of it, and the dry porridge fell out onto the floor. Wallace looked at the bottom of the box, 'Something's eaten a hole in this, too,' he thought, and then he looked at the cheese.

'Were you hungry in the night, Gromit?' called Wallace. 'Because someone's eaten my cheese.'

Gromit stood by the kitchen door and looked at Wallace. What was happening? Just then, the small sheep from the lorry walked behind Gromit. Gromit didn't see the sheep, but when he went back through the hall, he saw that there were no leaves on the plant. There were no leaves – and there was no plant!

Wallace went into the front room, picked up his newspaper, and sat down in his comfortable chair. 'I don't know. Something very strange is happening,' he said. When he opened the newspaper, he found a big hole in the middle of it. 'Something's eaten this, too,' he said.

Just then, the phone rang and Wallace picked it up. He didn't see the small sheep at his feet, and he said happily into the phone, 'Hello? Wallace and Gromit's Wash and Go Window Cleaning. Can we help you?'

Wallace heard a woman's voice at the other end of the phone; 'Hello. This is the wool shop in the High Street. My windows need a good clean. Can you come soon?'

'We'll come at once,' said Wallace, and he put the phone down.

'Time to go!' thought Gromit, and he pulled a lever in the wall which started the *Getting-Ready-to-Leave* machine. Wallace's chair moved up through a hole in the bedroom floor, then it moved back and dropped Wallace through a hole in a picture on the wall. Wallace's feet dropped into his black work shoes, then the machine turned, and he fell head first into his white **helmet**. After that, the machine put Wallace's window cleaning things into his hands, and dropped him into his blue work clothes. Then it put Wallace onto his **motorbike**, and pushed the motorbike up through the garage floor. Gromit came through a door from the kitchen, got into the **side-car**, and put on his helmet. Then the machine turned the motorbike round, put a **ladder** on the side of the side-car, and opened the garage doors.

After that, the machine started the motorbike, and Wallace and Gromit drove out of the garage, down the garden and into the street.

helmet you wear this hard hat to stop your head from getting hurt

motorbike a bicycle with a motor like a car that can go very fast

side-car a small car with wheels but no motor that goes next to a motorbike; a passenger can sit here

ladder you use this for climbing up or down tall buildings or other things

READING CHECK

Are these sentences true or false? Tick the boxes.

		True	False
a	A small sheep arrives at 62 West Wallaby Street in the middle of the night.	☑	☐
b	Everyone in the house is asleep when the sheep arrives.	☐	☐
c	'Lots of wool in the shops,' says the newspaper headline.	☐	☐
d	The porridge gun goes wrong and Wallace gets porridge all over his face.	☐	☐
e	Something is eating everything in the house.	☐	☐
f	Wallace and Gromit find the small sheep.	☐	☐
g	A woman from the wool shop sends a letter to Wallace.	☐	☐
h	Wallace and Gromit go to clean the windows of the wool shop.	☐	☐

WORD WORK

1 These words don't match the pictures. Correct them.

a ~~motorbike~~ *wool*   **b** plant **c** ladder **d** sign

e porridge **f** side-car **g** helmet **h** wool

6

2 Find words in the pieces of cheese to complete the sentences.

a There are a lot of m <u>achines</u> in Wallace's house.

shamnice

b Gromit loves k _ _ _ _ _ _ _ things.

nikingitt

c Wallace and Gromit's job is c _ _ _ _ _ _ _ _ windows.

gnilecna

d The small sheep escapes from a green l _ _ _ _ _ .

rolyr

e The porridge gun goes wrong because the sheep has eaten through half of the w _ _ _ .

rewi

f Gromit hits a b _ _ _ _ _ on the *Porridge Machine* to turn it off.

totubn

g Gromit uses a l _ _ _ _ to turn on the *Getting-Ready-to-Leave* machine.

reely

GUESS WHAT

What happens in the next chapter? Tick four boxes.

a ☐ Wallace cleans the wool shop windows.

b ☐ Gromit cleans the wool shop windows.

c ☐ Wallace talks to the woman at the wool shop.

d ☐ Wallace tells the woman that he loves her.

e ☐ Gromit sees another dog.

f ☐ Wallace wants to buy some wool from the shop.

g ☐ Wallace finds that there is no wool in the wool shop.

Chapter 2

At the wool shop

Wallace and Gromit arrived on their motorbike in front of the wool shop in the High Street. Gromit took the ladder off the side-car, and put one end of it into a **drain** in the street. He held on to the other end of the ladder and went up into the **air** with it. The top of the ladder flew up, and **landed** against the wall, next to the shop sign:

Gromit was now standing at the top of the ladder, and he was looking in through a window to a room on the first floor. Inside the room he could see a very big **guard dog**. The dog looked out of the window at Gromit, angrily.

'Time to start work,' thought Gromit.

He **tied** one end of an **elastic rope** to the sign and put the other end round his middle. Then he jumped off the ladder and **hung** with his head down and his feet in the air. As he moved up and down on the elastic rope he started cleaning the shop window.

drain dirty water goes down here

air the space above and around things

land to come down to the floor or to hit something

guard dog a dog that stops people attacking a place or a person

tie to keep something in place with string or rope

elastic a thin string that gets longer and shorter very easily

rope a very thick, strong string

hang (*past* **hung**) to hold onto something and be above the ground

While Gromit was cleaning the window, Wallace looked into the shop. Inside, there were lots of balls of wool in different colours. And there was also a woman, with short brown hair and big dark eyes. It was Wendolene, and the wool shop belonged to her. Wallace couldn't stop looking at Wendolene. She was knitting when he first saw her, but when she looked up and saw Wallace looking at her through the shop window, she put down her knitting. Then she smiled, and **waved** at Wallace.

'You need some wool, don't you, Gromit?' said Wallace, and he walked into the shop.

Now the unfriendly guard dog was sitting on a chair in the corner of the shop, and he was reading a newspaper. The headline on the front page said:

MORE SHEEP THIEVES

'Thank you for coming so quickly,' Wendolene said to Wallace.

Wallace looked around the shop and saw a sign on the wall next to some balls of wool, which said;

Only two balls of wool for each person

Without thinking, Wallace took a red ball from the bottom of the **pile** and the other balls fell onto the floor.

'Oh dear,' he said, and he went down on his hands on the floor to **pick up** the wool.

'Oh, don't worry. I can do that!' said Wendolene.

A ball of wool **rolled** across the floor and stopped at the guard dog's feet. Wallace came over to pick it up. The dog looked at Wallace over the top of his newspaper.

'This is Preston,' said the woman. 'He's my dog.'

'Good dog!' said Wallace, and put his hand on Preston's head. Preston didn't look very happy.

wave to move your hand in the air

pile a number of things one on top of the other

pick up to take something in your hand

roll to move by turning over and over

9

'I'm very sorry. I can pick everything up,' said Wallace worriedly. 'I won't be a minute.' And he started to pick up the wool again.

Now Wendolene was down on the floor and was picking up balls of wool, too. There was a red ball of wool in the middle of the floor. Wendolene's hand went to pick it up, and Wallace's hand went to pick it up, too. By mistake, Wallace put his hand on her hand.

'Oh,' he said.

'Oh,' said Wendolene.

They looked at each other for some time.

'Er . . . What did you want?' Wendolene asked Wallace in the end.

'I, er, well . . . ,' began Wallace. He felt very stupid and he didn't know what to say.

Preston put down his newspaper and walked out of the shop. Gromit was still hanging on the elastic rope but he wasn't moving up and down any more. Preston went over and pulled Gromit's helmet off. Gromit started **bouncing** up and down again on his elastic ropes. He couldn't do anything to stop himself.

Back in the wool shop, Wallace and Wendolene were talking.

'My name's Wendolene,' said the woman, 'Wendolene Ramsbottom.'

'Oh, that's nice!' said Wallace. 'I'm Wallace, the window cleaner. Is this your shop?'

bounce to move quickly up and down like a ball hitting the ground again and again

'Yes. It was my father's shop, but he left it to me when he died.'

Wendolene looked at a picture on the wall. There was a nice old man in it. He had wild white hair and was wearing a white coat. In the picture with him was Preston, the dog.

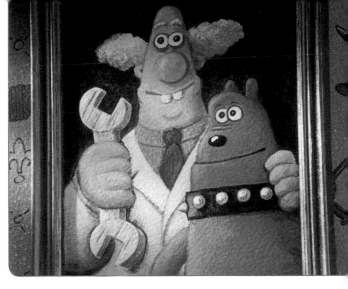

'He left me Preston, too. Preston is my guard dog,' explained Wendolene. 'But he didn't leave me much money. He spent it all **inventing** things.'

'Really? I'm an inventor myself,' said Wallace.

'Oh!' said Wendolene.

Wallace looked down and saw Preston's newspaper on the chair. He read the headline on the front of it.

'The police still haven't caught those sheep thieves, I see,' he said. 'But you've got a lot of wool in your shop.'

Wendolene didn't reply. She looked away quickly.

'Your dog's waiting,' she said.

It was true. Gromit was waiting outside for Wallace. His elastic rope wasn't moving up and down now, and he was hanging with his feet in the air and his head down.

'Right, I'll get him,' said Wallace, and he gave Wendolene all the balls of wool in his hands.

Wendolene stood with her arms round the balls of wool, and looked at the nice clean shop windows.

'Oh, they're very clean. You've done a great job.'

'Windows are our business,' said Wallace.

Then he turned round to leave the shop, and walked into the nice clean glass door.

invent to make or think of something for the first time

11

READING CHECK

Match the first and second parts of these sentences.

a Gromit stays outside the wool shop and . . .

b Wallace goes into the shop to . . .

c Preston the dog is reading a newspaper . . .

d The newspaper headline says that . . .

e A sign in the shop says that each person can . . .

f The balls of wool fall to the floor and . . .

g Preston goes out of the shop and . . .

h Wendolene's father was an inventor but . . .

1 Wallace and Wendolene pick them up.

2 cleans the windows.

3 get wool for Gromit.

4 pulls Gromit's helmet off.

5 there's a problem with sheep thieves.

6 he didn't have much money.

7 buy only two balls of wool.

8 when Wallace goes into the shop.

WORD WORK

1 Use the verbs in the ball of wool to complete the sentences.

a When is this plane going to ....land...... in Rome? I have another plane to catch there.

b As the train left, he looked out of the window and began to .... goodbye to his family.

bounce   hang
invent   land   pick up
roll   tie   wave

c The guard decided to .... the thief's hands and feet with some rope.

d When did Alexander Graham Bell .... the telephone?

e Don't leave your coat on the chair; you can .... it behind the door.

f Your ball is going to .... down the hill if you leave it there.

g I couldn't catch the ball and it started to .... across the road.

h I've got a very bad back, so I can't .... heavy things.

2 Correct the boxed words in the sentences. They all come from Chapter 2.

a This skirt has got plastic round the top so it doesn't need any buttons.

...elastic...

b There's a terrible smell coming from the train outside the kitchen. ....

c I don't like travelling by aid, I prefer travelling by bus or by boat. ....

d All your clean clothes are in a pine in the cupboard. ....

e He climbed down from a third floor window using a dope. ....

f At night they have gourd digs at the factory. ....

GUESS WHAT

What happens in the next chapter? Tick the boxes.

a Preston the dog goes to visit . . .

   1 ☐ 62 West Wallaby Street.

   2 ☐ a dog food factory.

   3 ☐ a friend.

b Wallace and Gromit go home and find
. . . there.

   1 ☐ Wendolene

   2 ☐ Preston the dog

   3 ☐ the small sheep

c Wallace uses a new . . . machine.

   1 ☐ knitting

   2 ☐ hair-washing

   3 ☐ window-cleaning

d The machine . . .

   1 ☐ works well.

   2 ☐ goes wrong.

   3 ☐ breaks down.

Chapter 3

Wallace's Knitting Machine

Preston the guard dog arrived at West Wallaby Street. He went round to the back of Wallace and Gromit's house. There was a piece of sheep's wool hanging by their back door, and he smelled it carefully.

Just then, Preston heard Wallace's motorbike in the street. Wallace and Gromit were coming home after their window-cleaning visit to the wool shop. Preston didn't want them to see him, so he quickly looked for a place to hide. He saw a door, opened it, and went through it down into the **cellar** under the house. There he hid under a drain **cover** in the cellar floor.

Soon after that Wallace and Gromit went into the house. 'Let's have a nice cup of tea,' said Wallace. But he stopped suddenly at the door of the front room and he looked around. It was terrible! Everything was untidy, and there were big holes everywhere – in the chairs, in the carpets, even in the pictures on the wall.

cellar a room under the ground at the bottom of a house

cover this goes on top of something

'Oh no! What's all this?' said Wallace. 'Is it thieves?'

Gromit heard a noise from the kitchen and he went to see what it was. When he opened the kitchen door, he saw a small sheep. It was the sheep from the lorry. It was standing in the middle of the kitchen with Gromit's **bone** in its mouth. Everything in the kitchen was untidy;

there was food from the cupboard all over the floor, and there was food all over the sheep, too.

'I've never seen anything like it, Gromit!' said Wallace, walking down the hall. Then he came into the kitchen.

'Look at that!' he said, surprised to see a sheep in his kitchen. Gromit was looking angrily at the sheep, but Wallace went on in a friendly way.

'Look, the poor little thing's really hungry. Come here, **lad**. Don't be afraid.'

Wallace looked at the sheep's dirty white wool coat. Then he picked up the sheep and said, 'We must give you a wash.'

At once Wallace took the sheep out of the kitchen and down some stairs into the cellar. Gromit went after them.

There was a big machine in the middle of the cellar. It had a sign on it which said: *Wallace's Knitting Machine*. There was a big bath next to the machine and Wallace carefully put the sheep into it.

'Now, there's nothing to worry about,' he said. 'You're going to have a quick wash. Gromit's had a wash in this bath, haven't you, Gromit?'

Gromit moved his head up and down unhappily. 'And it was terrible,' he thought.

bone a hard white thing inside an animal's body

lad young man

Gromit pushed some buttons and turned a **dial** on the machine to *Wash*.

'Right, let's start then,' said Wallace, and the machine started washing the sheep.

Wallace and Gromit did not know that all this time Preston was hiding in a drain under the cellar floor. From under the drain cover Preston was watching and listening to everything that was happening in the cellar.

Suddenly a red light on Wallace's machine started going on and off. 'Oh no, there's something wrong with it!' thought Gromit. The machine dial suddenly moved from *Wash* to ***Light Shave***.

'Oh, dear!' said Wallace.

Now the machine **sucked** the sheep from the bath into a **dryer** above their heads. The dryer **blew** warm air onto the sheep, and then it blew the sheep down into the *Knitting Machine*.

'Oh! Do something, Gromit!' cried Wallace, but Gromit couldn't do anything.

'Oh no, we can't stop it now,' said Wallace.

Lots of arms were moving in and out of the *Knitting Machine*, and on the end of each arm there were **clippers**. The clippers were going in and out of the machine very

dial a round, flat thing that you turn to make a machine work

light shave when a man cuts the hair from his face, but not very carefully

suck to take moving air into something

dryer a machine that makes wet clothes dry

blow (*past* **blew, blown**) to push moving air out of something

clippers a small machine that you use to cut hair short on a sheep or a man's head

quickly. They were busy cutting the wool from the sheep's back! At the same time, wool was coming out from the other side of the machine. The wool was different colours: red, blue and green.

'Turn it off, Gromit. Oh dear,' cried Wallace.

The *Knitting Machine* started knitting the new wool into a little **pullover**. When the pullover was ready, the machine put it onto Wallace's head. Wallace moved his head around, but he couldn't see a thing.

'It's great, Gromit!' he said. 'But it's too small for me.'

Just then, Wallace and Gromit heard a little noise from inside the machine.

'Baa,' cried the sheep.

'Ah, good. He's alive!' thought Gromit.

Wallace pulled the pullover off his head and just then, a door in the side of the machine opened, and the sheep came out. 'Baa!' he cried again.

'He looks OK to me!' said Wallace. But the sheep didn't have his warm wool coat now, and he was very cold. Wallace picked him up. 'He needs a name. Let's call him Shaun,' he said to Gromit. 'Come on Shaun.'

Wallace carried Shaun upstairs into the kitchen, and Gromit followed them.

At the top of the stairs, Gromit stopped and listened. Was that a noise?

'Is there someone in the cellar?' he thought for a minute. 'No, there's nothing,' he decided in the end, and he closed the cellar door and followed Wallace to the kitchen.

But there was someone in the cellar – Preston! When he was sure that he was alone, he pushed up the drain cover and climbed out of his hiding place. He went over to the table, and looked at Wallace's plans for making the *Knitting Machine*. 'Very interesting,' he thought. Then he picked up the plans and took them away with him.

pullover
something warm and made of wool that you wear over a shirt

READING CHECK

Put these sentences in the correct order. Number them 1–9.

a ☐ Gromit finds a dirty sheep in the kitchen.

b ☐ Wallace and Gromit come back home on their motorbike.

c ☐ Preston arrives at Wallace and Gromit's house.

d ☐ Preston goes into the cellar and hides there.

e ☐ Preston takes the plans for Wallace's machine.

f ☐ Wallace takes the sheep to the cellar.

g ☐ The machine makes a little pullover with the sheep's wool.

h ☐ Wallace puts the sheep into a bath next to the knitting machine to give it a wash.

i ☐ The machine goes wrong and cuts off the sheep's wool.

WORD WORK

1 Find eleven words from Chapter 3 in Gromit's bone.

blowbonescellarclipperscoverdialdryerladlightshavepulloversucks

2 Complete the sentences with the words from Activity 1.

a 'It's cold in here.'

'Why don't you put on a ..pullover... ?'

b How does your radio work? Is there a .... to turn or a button to push?

c He isn't an old man. He's a young ....

d 'This coffee is very hot.'

'Well, ... on it to make it colder.'

e 'Do you want me to cut your hair short?'

'Yes. With ...., please.'

f I don't have a lot of hair on my face, so I only want a ....

....

g Some people have a ... . under their house. It's a good place for keeping things.

h When the washing machine finishes, take the clothes out and put them in the

....

i When it rains, I put a .... over my motorbike so it stays dry.

j We've got a new machine for the garden; it .... all the leaves from the ground in autumn.

k Be careful when you eat the fish – there are lots of .... in it.

GUESS WHAT

What happens in the next chapter? Write *Yes* or *No*.

a Wallace and Gromit have another cleaning job. ....

b Wallace visits Wendolene at her shop. ....

c Preston takes Shaun away in his lorry. ....

d Preston takes Gromit away in his lorry. ....

e Wallace and Wendolene decide to get married. ....

Chapter 4

Gromit investigates

Gromit was sitting down and reading the newspaper with interest. The headline on the front page said:

POLICE LOOKING FOR SHEEP KILLER

Shaun was next to Gromit. He was wearing the pullover from the *Knitting Machine* and eating some of the newspaper. Then he walked over and took a piece of cheese from Wallace's plate. Wallace was mending the porridge gun.

'Gromit, you know that we're cleaning the town clock tomorrow,' said Wallace. 'I think we can use the *Porridge Machine* for that job.'

The next day Wallace and Gromit went to clean the town clock in the High Street. Shaun went with them. Gromit climbed up the ladder to the clock face. In the street below, Wallace put some **soap** in the porridge gun and shot it at the clock face, but some of the soap hit Gromit in the face.

soap you wash things with this

'Sorry Gromit. That was too soapy,' called Wallace.

Gromit cleaned the soap from his face and Wallace shot some soap at the clock face again. This time the gun worked well.

'I'll see you in a minute, Gromit,' said Wallace. 'I'm not going to be long.'

Wallace walked over to the wool shop and went in. Shaun followed him, but the sheep didn't go into the wool shop. **Instead** he walked through a large open **gate** into the back **yard** behind the shop. Gromit was watching Wallace and Shaun from the top of the ladder. Suddenly he saw Preston. Wendolene's guard dog was standing at an upstairs window. He was looking out of the window at something. 'What's Preston looking at? I'll finish cleaning and then I'll go and **investigate**,' thought Gromit.

In the wool shop, Wallace was talking to Wendolene. 'I just thought I'd come and see you . . . ,' he said to her. Wendolene looked at him with her big dark eyes.

'Tell me about the window cleaning,' she said.

'Well, it's only for a short time, you understand,' said Wallace.

'Oh really?' said Wendolene.

'Yes, I invent things most of the time,' said Wallace. 'But . . .'

'Oh, what kind of things do you invent?' asked Wendolene.

'Well, different things . . .' began Wallace.

'It's so sad that Daddy never met you,' said Wendolene. 'Poor Daddy.'

instead in the place of something

gate an outside door into a yard, field, or garden

yard an empty square behind a house; like a garden but with no trees or flowers

investigate to find out about something

Gromit finished cleaning the clock face and climbed down the ladder. Then he walked over to the wool shop and started to clean the shop window. Suddenly he heard Shaun's voice. Shaun was looking out of a hole in the wall above him. 'Baa!' said Shaun, and then he pulled his head in again.

'What's Shaun doing up there?' thought Gromit. He climbed up the ladder and put his head through the hole in the wall. It was dark inside, and Gromit couldn't see very well. He tried to touch Shaun and then someone suddenly took a photograph of the two of them together.

'Strange,' thought Gromit, and he pulled his head out of the hole in the wall. 'I must go and investigate. I must see what's happening in that room above the shop.'

Gromit climbed down the ladder, and walked through the shop. Wallace was still busy talking to Wendolene, and neither of them saw him.

'Of all the women that I've ever met . . . ,' Wallace was saying. 'And there haven't been many women in my life, you understand . . .'

Gromit walked past them and went upstairs. He opened the door to the room above the shop and went in. The room was empty. He picked up an empty dog food **tin** from the floor. '*Preston's Dog Food*,' it said on the front. Then he saw a strange picture of a **butcher** on the wall. He had a big meat cutter in his hand, but he didn't have a face; there was just a hole in the wall instead.

tin a metal box for food or drink

butcher a man who sells meat

Suddenly Gromit heard a noise from the back yard. 'Baa! Baa!' It was Shaun! Gromit looked out of the back window and saw a big green lorry in the back yard. He could see Shaun, too. His little head was looking through a hole in the side of the lorry. Gromit ran downstairs and hurried past Wallace and Wendolene in the shop.

Wallace was still speaking to Wendolene, 'So you see. I'm trying to say . . . in a way . . .'

Neither of them saw Gromit. He ran out into the back yard and he went to the lorry. Very quietly Gromit pulled the lever on the back of the lorry, and opened the back door. Lots of sheep ran out of the back of the lorry. They ran across the back yard, and into the shop.

Wallace was still speaking to Wendolene, 'Of the women that I've met, you . . . er . . .' He took Wendolene's hand in his hand, and just then, all the sheep ran through the shop like a crowd of people hurrying through a train station. Wallace couldn't hold on to Wendolene's hand for long because the sheep carried him away on their woolly backs and out into the street.

'Shall we meet again? The same time next week?' Wallace called to Wendolene. He was holding onto the ladder now, but the white river of sheep soon carried him far away down the street.

Gromit was still looking for Shaun. He didn't know that Preston was sitting in the driver's seat of the lorry and was watching everything, and waiting. Gromit found Shaun in the back of the lorry with ropes round him to stop him escaping. Gromit **untied** him, and at once Shaun started to climb out of the lorry. Just then, Preston pulled a lever and closed the back of the lorry. At the last minute Shaun jumped out, just before the door closed. But it was too late for Gromit to escape. He was still in the back of the lorry when Preston quickly drove it away with a big bad smile on his face.

untie to take off ropes that tie someone

READING CHECK

Correct the mistakes in these sentences.

a Gromit ~~breaks~~ *washes* the clock in the town square.

b Shaun goes into the back yard behind the book shop.

c Wallace talks to Wendolene in the street.

d Shaun puts his foot out of a hole in the wall above the shop.

e Gromit climbs a ladder and puts his arm through the hole.

f Someone takes a photo of Preston and Shaun.

g Gromit climbs down, walks through the shop, and goes to the room under it.

h Gromit finds an empty tin of *Preston's Cat Food* in the empty room.

i Gromit sees Shaun looking out of a red lorry.

j All the cows from the lorry run through the shop and into the street.

k Wendolene helps Shaun to escape from the lorry.

l Preston drives away with Wendolene in the lorry.

WORD WORK

1 Complete the crossword with eight words from Chapter 4.

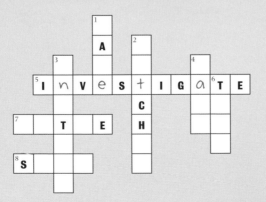

2 Use the words from Activity 1 to complete the sentences.

a I heard a noise in the cellar. I'm going to ..investigate.. .

b We haven't got a garden, but my little brother often plays in the .... behind the house.

c Someone forgot to close the .... when they left the field. All the sheep are in the road now!

d The dogs are hungry. Have you got any .... of dog food for them?

e My uncle is a ...., he sells very good meat and his shop is always busy.

f Help! Can you .... this rope for me? Someone's tied me to the chair.

g Do you want tea, or would you like coffee .... ?

h You need to use .... when you wash your hands if you want them to be really clean.

GUESS WHAT

What happens in the next chapter? Match the parts of the sentences.

a Shaun . . .

b Wendolene . . .

c Wallace . . .

1 goes to prison for killing sheep.

2 can't believe that Gromit is a sheep killer.

d Gromit . . .

3 comes to say sorry to Wallace.

4 climbs up to Gromit's window to help him escape.

Chapter 5

Gromit's in trouble

Wallace was at home in the front room, and he was reading the newspaper. The headline on the front page said:

POLICE CATCH SHEEP KILLER

Under the headline there was a big photograph of Gromit. In the photograph, Gromit was holding a big meat cutter over Shaun's neck! It was the photograph from the room above the wool shop.

'Gromit's in trouble now. They caught him killing sheep!' said Wallace. 'Killing sheep's a crime. They'll send him to prison for this, I'm sure.'

But Wallace wasn't alone at number 62 West Wallaby Street. His house was full of the sheep from the lorry. Just then, two of them took the newspaper that Wallace was reading in their mouths, pulled it into pieces, and ate it.

'Hey! Stop that!' cried Wallace.

Suddenly there was a ring at the front door.

'Move!' said Wallace, and he pushed past all the sheep in the front room. He pushed past more sheep in the hall and opened the front door. Wendolene was standing there.

'I'm so sorry,' she said.

'Er, sorry for what?' asked Wallace.

'I can't say,' answered Wendolene. 'Listen, please stay away from me. Stay away from my shop, and from its stupid, stupid windows.'

'I . . . Well, I . . . ,' said Wallace.

'Forget me. I'm no good for you,' said Wendolene. She took out a **handkerchief** from her coat, put it to her face and started to cry. 'I'm very sorry about Gromit,' she said, and she turned her back to Wallace and cried into her handkerchief. Wallace stood in the hall full of sheep and watched Wendolene walk away slowly down the street. Why was she sorry? He didn't understand.

The next morning, a sheep **bit** a rope that went to the lever of the *Getting-Up-In-The-Morning* machine, and it went wrong.

Wallace fell down very quickly through the bedroom floor and into the room below. 'Ow!' cried Wallace.

The next minute, two big sheep fell through the same hole and landed on the breakfast table in front of him. Instead of his shirt and his pullover, the machine dropped a third sheep on top of him.

'Hmm,' said Wallace.

Just then, another sheep put the morning paper on a chair next to Wallace. Wallace picked up the paper and read it at once. The headline said:

DOG EXPLAINS ALL TO POLICE

'Oh, Gromit!' said Wallace.

That afternoon, Wallace read the afternoon paper.

"GROMIT BIT ME," SAYS MAN

One of the sheep was standing behind Wallace, and it was reading the paper, too. 'Oh Gromit!' said Wallace for the second time that day.

That evening, Wallace read the evening paper.

GROMIT GOES TO PRISON FOR LIFE

handkerchief you cry into this

bite (*past* **bit**, **bitten**) to cut something with your teeth

All the sheep in the living room were standing behind Wallace now, and they were all reading the paper, too. 'Oh Gromit,' cried Wallace sadly for the third time. All the sheep that were standing around him cried sadly, too. Wallace looked up at the photo on the sitting room wall. All the sheep around him looked up at it, too. The photo showed Wallace smiling, with Gromit at his side. Wallace felt very sad. What was his good old friend Gromit doing now?

Gromit was lying on his prison bed. He was reading a book about prison life by the famous Russian writer dog, Fido Dogstoevsky. Someone pushed a bowl of dog food through a hole in the door. Gromit looked at the food, but he wasn't hungry. Then the hole in the door opened again and someone pushed a **parcel** into Gromit's prison room.

Gromit quickly got up from his bed and went to pick up the parcel. He untied the parcel and found a **puzzle** inside it. It was a picture puzzle in a box with 5,000 pieces. The picture on the front of the box showed lots of white sheep with blue faces. 'Oh no!' thought Gromit. 'Not sheep!' And he put his head in his hands and cried.

parcel a paper box with things in

puzzle a picture in many pieces that you must put together

Later that night, when the moon was up in the sky, Gromit finished the puzzle. When he put the last piece into place, he looked down at the finished puzzle on the table in front of him, and he had a surprise. There was the picture of the blue and white sheep, but there were some red words on the puzzle, too. They said:

Friday night. 8 p.m. Be ready. A friend.

Gromit looked at the **calendar** on the prison wall. It was Friday today. He picked up the red clock by his bed and looked at it. It was eight o'clock. Then Gromit looked up at his window and there was Shaun with a **metal**-cutter. Shaun wanted to help Gromit escape. He quickly cut through the metal **bars** and helped Gromit to get out through the window.

Outside the prison Shaun was standing on top of ten other sheep. Each sheep had its feet on the **shoulders** of the sheep below it. At the bottom of all the sheep stood Wallace. Wallace was holding up all the sheep on his shoulders to make a ladder for Gromit to escape down. Suddenly Wallace stood on a piece of soap on the ground. He **slipped** and fell on his back. At once all the sheep, and Gromit, fell down on top of him.

'Aargh! Oooh,' cried Wallace.

calendar a book with all the days of the year in it, often with a different month on every page

metal gold and silver are expensive metals; iron is a cheaper metal

bar a strong metal stick that goes across a prison window to stop prisoners escaping

shoulder this is between your arm and your neck

slip to move very quickly on something wet

READING CHECK

Complete these sentences with the correct names. You can use each name more than once.

Gromit

Shaun

Wallace

Wendolene

a Lots of sheep are living with
...Wallace... .

b .... comes to say sorry to
....

c .... reads the latest news
about .... in the morning,
afternoon and evening newspapers.

d Someone sends .... a
parcel in prison.

e .... finds a note from a
friend on the puzzle.

f At eight o'clock .... looks
up and sees .... at his
prison window.

g ...., ... and
ten sheep have come to help
.... escape.

WORD WORK

1 These words don't match the pictures. Correct them.

handkerchief
a ~~shoulder~~

b metal bars

c slip

d bite

e handkerchief

f calendar

g parcel

h puzzle

2 Use words from Activity 1 in the correct form to complete the sentences about the story.

a The newspapers say that Gromit bit a man and that he is a sheep killer.

b Wendolene comes to say sorry to Gromit and she cries into her
_ a _ _ _ _ _ c _ _ _ _ .

c 'Friday Night. 8 p.m. Be ready. A friend,' say the words on Gromit's _ u _ _ _ e.

d The sheep climb on top of Wallace's s _ _ _ _ _ _ rs to make a ladder.

e Shaun cuts the _ a _ _ in front of Gromit's prison window with a _ e _ a _-cutter.

f Wallace stands on some soap, and _ l _ _ _ .

GUESS WHAT

What happens in the next chapter? Tick three boxes.

a ☐ The police find Gromit and take him back to prison.

b ☐ Wallace and Gromit find the real sheep thieves.

c ☐ Preston puts Shaun and lots of other sheep in the back of his lorry.

d ☐ Wallace and Gromit follow Preston's lorry on the motorbike.

e ☐ Wendolene steals Wallace's *Knitting Machine*.

Chapter 6

The real sheep thieves

It was the middle of the night and very dark. Wallace and Gromit were now far away from the prison. They were sitting on the ground by a wall in the country. They were next to a gate, and on the other side of the gate there was a field. The sheep were in the field, and they were eating the **grass** there happily.

'You must leave the country now, you know,' said Wallace. 'You're running away from the police,' he went on. 'They'll come to look for you.'

Suddenly a big lorry drove off the road. It drove past Wallace and Gromit, crashed through the gate, and stopped in the field. Wallace looked over the wall. Two people were getting out of the lorry. It was Wendolene and her guard dog, Preston!

'Wendol—' cried Wallace when he saw her, but Gromit pulled him back behind the wall, and stopped him from calling her name.

grass it is green; gardens and fields have lots of it on the ground

Wendolene was wearing a dark coat, and she was carrying a big stick. Preston was wearing a small black hat. He opened the back of the lorry and Wendolene blew loudly on a **whistle**. She held the stick out in front of her

and the sheep started to walk across the field one behind the other. They were walking straight into the lorry.

'So Preston and Wendolene are the sheep thieves!' thought Gromit.

Gromit pushed Wallace into another field. There was an old **scarecrow** there, and Wallace and Gromit quickly put on its clothes. Then they looked over the wall into the field with the lorry. Wendolene and Preston couldn't see or hear them, but Wallace and Gromit could see and hear everything. They were watching and listening very carefully.

Nearly all the sheep were in the lorry now. Just then, Preston saw Shaun in a corner of the field. He went over to the small sheep. Shaun couldn't stop shaking; he didn't want to go into the lorry. Preston started **growling** at Shaun.

whistle something that makes a high musical noise when you blow into it

scarecrow a figure in old clothes that people put in fields to make birds afraid so they don't come and eat fruit or vegetables there

growl to make a deep, angry noise

'Stop it! Stop it, Preston!' cried Wendolene. She hit Preston with her stick, and knocked his hat off. 'We can't go on like this. We must stop stealing sheep,' Wendolene went on. 'It wasn't so bad when we took only the wool. I need wool for my shop. But this is **evil**.'

But Preston didn't listen to Wendolene. He took her stick and broke it into two pieces.

'Oh no! What are you doing, Preston?' she cried. 'Daddy didn't make you for this.'

Preston pushed her into the back of the lorry with the sheep.

'Your job is to make things **safe** for me!' cried Wendolene, but Preston pushed Shaun into her arms, and closed the back of the lorry.

'Help. Let me out! You're not going to make me into dog food,' cried Wendolene.

Preston climbed into the driver's seat, and started the lorry. 'Dog food!' cried Wallace. 'So that's what Preston is doing with the sheep. He's killing them to make dog food!! I must do something.'

evil very bad
safe not dangerous

Preston was already driving the lorry out of the field and down the dark road. Wallace and Gromit took off their scarecrow clothes as quickly as possible. Wallace started the motorbike and Gromit jumped into the side-car, and they drove away quickly after the lorry. 'Don't worry, Wendolene,' Wallace shouted. 'We're on our way!'

They drove along the dark road and went past a dark old garage, but they couldn't see the big lorry in front of them any more. Where were Preston, Wendolene, Shaun, and the other sheep now? 'We've lost them!' said Wallace.

Suddenly the lorry turned on its lights again and drove out of the old garage and back onto the road. Now the lorry was behind Wallace and Gromit's motorbike. Wallace looked back – the lorry was getting nearer and nearer. Preston was driving faster and faster. The front of the lorry began to hit the back of the motorbike again and again.

'Oooh! I can't go any faster!' cried Wallace.

Gromit suddenly had an **idea**. He took the ladder from the side of the motorbike and put one end in front of Wallace. Then he climbed up to the top of the ladder and caught some telephone wires in his hands. The motorbike went up in the air, flew round in a circle, and landed back on the road behind the big lorry. They were safe again. Gromit climbed down the ladder, and got back into the side-car. Just then, the side-car broke away from the motorbike. 'Oh, no!' cried Wallace.

idea a plan or a new thought

2,000 feet 609.6
metres

propeller this
goes round and
round on the front
of a plane, and
makes it fly

Gromit couldn't stop the side-car! The motorbike followed the road and went to the right, but the side-car went straight on. It went off the road and hit a sign. The sign broke away in Gromit's hands, and he read it as he went along in the side-car.

DANGER

**2,000 feet
to the bottom**

The side-car started to fall. Soon it was falling faster and faster.

'I'm going to crash!' thought Gromit.

Quickly he pushed some buttons at the front of the side-car. Wings came out of the sides, and a **propeller** came out of the front. The side-car changed into a plane and flew up into the sky.

Gromit was out of danger! But what was happening to the motorbike and the lorry on the road?

Wallace was driving fast behind the lorry now. He was very near the back of it. Wendolene looked out worriedly and saw him.

rescue to save somebody from danger

'Wallace, help me!' called Wendolene from the lorry.

'Don't worry Wendolene!' cried Wallace. 'I'm coming to **rescue** you.'

The ladder was still on the motorbike in front of Wallace, and he climbed up to the top of it. With heavy Wallace now at the top, the ladder fell onto the back of the lorry.

Wallace wasn't driving the motorbike, but he could hold onto the lorry. And he was trying to open the back door.

At last, he pulled a lever at the back of the lorry, and the back door fell open.

With the door now open, Wallace found himself suddenly face down. He was dangerously near the road. He was holding onto the back door of the lorry, and his feet were on the ladder. He was making a bridge from the back of the lorry to the motorbike.

Shaun the sheep looked out of the back of the lorry and walked quickly down the open door to Wallace.

What was he doing? Did he want to pull Wallace into the lorry? Or did he have a different plan in his head?

'Be careful, Shaun!' called Wendolene.

READING CHECK

Correct nine more mistakes in the story.

It's the middle of the ~~day~~ *night*, and Wallace and Gromit are sitting in the country. Suddenly

Wendolene and Preston arrive in a car. Wallace and Gromit hide behind a door.

Wendolene and Preston get all the cows from the field and put them into the back of

the lorry. They are the sheep thieves!

Wendolene wants Preston to stop taking the sheep. Preston breaks her hat and

puts her in the front of the lorry together with Shaun. He is taking them to his cat food

factory.

Wallace and Gromit drive down the road after the lorry. Suddenly the lorry is behind

them, and it's coming nearer and nearer. How can they escape it? Using telephone

books Gromit finds a way to put their motorbike behind the lorry again.

When Gromit's side-car breaks away from the motorbike, it changes into a boat and

he escapes safely. Wallace uses a scarecrow and makes a bridge from the back of the

lorry to his motorbike with it.

WORD WORK

Match the words in the lorry with the underlined words in the sentences.

> evil   grass   growls   idea   propeller
> rescue   safe   ~~scarecrow~~   whistles

a Wallace and Gromit hide in clothes that belong to a <u>figure to make birds afraid</u>.
scarecrow

b Sheep often eat <u>a green plant covering the ground</u>. ....

c Wendolene <u>makes a musical noise</u>, and the sheep go into the lorry. ....

d When Preston sees Shaun, he <u>makes a deep angry noise</u>. ....

e Wendolene thinks that taking sheep to make dog food is <u>very bad</u>. ....

f Wendolene's father wanted her to be <u>not in danger</u>, so he made Preston.
....

g Gromit has a good <u>plan</u> that helps them to escape from Preston's lorry.
....

h Gromit's side-car gets wings and a <u>thing that goes round on the front</u>. ....

i Wallace wants to <u>take</u> Wendolene <u>away from something dangerous</u>. ....

GUESS WHAT

Who does what in the next chapter? Match each name with a sentence.

> Wallace   Gromit   Wendolene   Preston   Shaun

a .... is the first to leave the lorry and get onto the motorbike.

b .... catches all the sheep in the lorry again.

c Preston drives .... and .... into his factory with all the sheep.

d .... flies into the factory to save his friends.

Chapter 7

To the rescue

Wallace was still holding onto the back door of the lorry with his arms, and at the same time he was holding onto the ladder with his feet. Shaun the sheep was walking **towards** him. Then Shaun walked over his back and along the ladder onto the motorbike. At once, all the other sheep in the lorry started to follow Shaun.

'Wait a minute! One by one!' cried Wallace.

One by one, all the sheep walked down the back door of the lorry, over Wallace's back, and along the ladder onto the motorbike. With all the heavy sheep now on the motorbike, Wallace stopped holding on to the lorry, and the ladder went up into the air again with Wallace at the top of it.

'Stand on each other's shoulders down there!' cried Wallace, and the sheep stood on each other's shoulders below him. All the sheep in the middle held onto the ladder, and the sheep at the bottom drove the motorbike.

towards nearer

Gromit was flying in the side-car plane above them. He had the porridge gun in his plane and he put some porridge into it. Then he flew past the motorbike and waved to Wallace.

Wallace was still standing at the top of the ladder and he waved back to Gromit. Suddenly Wallace looked ahead and saw a **low** bridge on the road in front. The ladder was too tall to go under the bridge and the sheep were all holding onto the ladder.

'Careful, lads!' cried Wallace. All the sheep moved nearer to each other, Wallace dropped down a little, and they put the ladder **sideways**. That way, they all got under the bridge safely.

But Preston stopped the lorry suddenly on the other side of the bridge. Because the lorry had its back door down, the motorbike drove straight on and went into the back of the lorry before they could stop. Now Preston had all of them! He closed the back of the lorry and drove away with his prisoners inside.

low not high

sideways on one side; not straight

Gromit watched all this from high up in the air. He flew down low in his plane, and shot porridge at Preston in the front of the lorry. But Preston closed the window and went on driving. Gromit was following him through the town. Soon they arrived in the town square. Just in time, Gromit saw the town clock in front of him. 'Help!' he thought. 'I'm going to hit the clock!' At once he pulled the flying lever back and flew his plane up the side of the clock, high into the night sky, and away from Preston and the lorry.

Preston drove round to the back of the wool shop. There was a big sign for a bread shop in the yard behind the shop. When Preston drove near the sign, it opened in the middle, and Preston drove the lorry through. This was the secret gate into Preston's dog food factory. High up over the town square, Gromit turned his plane round, ready to go after Preston.

Now Wallace, Wendolene, Shaun and all the other sheep were prisoners inside the dog food factory. They were all standing in a large metal **wagon**. The wagon took them across the factory past a large *Knitting Machine*.

wagon a kind of open car that a train or machine pulls

'Where did you get that from?' asked Wallace. 'That's my machine!'

But the sign on the side said, *Preston's Knitting Machine*.

'You stole my invention!' said Wallace.

Preston pulled a lever, and Wallace, Wendolene and all the sheep fell out of the wagon into the big bath of the washing machine. But Shaun jumped out of the wagon on the other side, and escaped. The machine started to wash Wallace and Wendolene, and the sheep. Then Preston pushed a button, and a big **tube** came towards them. This tube sucked things up from the bath and took them to the dryer. The tube moved nearer and it began to suck Wallace into the dryer.

'Help . . . oh, Shaun! Help!' cried Wendolene.

tube a long thin thing that water or air can go through in a machine

'Where's Gromit?' cried Wallace.

'Shaun, do something! Help!' cried Wendolene.

At that moment, Gromit was still high up in the sky, but he was flying down quickly towards the secret factory behind the wool shop. As he was flying back down, he saw the words *Preston's Dog Food* in red lights on the side of the town clock.

'Oh, no! Preston's going to make them into dog food!'

remembered Gromit worriedly. 'Will I get there in time to rescue them?'

Gromit's plane flew lower and lower.

He flew down into the back yard and saw a big **wooden** door in front of him. There were big letters on the door saying *Preston's Dog Food*.

Gromit took off his helmet and **threw** it **away**. He didn't need it now!

wooden made of wood

throw away (*past* **threw, thrown**) you do this when you don't need something any longer and want to lose it

44

Quickly he pushed a green button in front of him, and the wings on his plane went into the sides of the side-car. The side-car crashed through the wooden door into the factory, and at once the plane wings came out again. What a clever dog!

Now there was a metal door in front of Gromit. Did this worry him? Of course it didn't. He pushed the green button in front of him, and the wings on his plane went in. The side-car crashed through the metal door, and at once the plane wings came out again. What a wonderful plane! Could nothing stop it?

Now there was a **brick** wall in front of him, but unluckily Gromit was too late this time. He didn't push the green button in time, and so the wings on his plane didn't go in. What a stupid mistake!

The plane crashed through the wall, and this time the wings broke off the side-car! What a terrible accident!

Now his plane had no wings, it was nothing more than a flying side-car! This was very bad news for Gromit.

How long could he stay in the air now? And how could he possibly land safely?

brick made of square stones for building houses

READING CHECK

What do they say or think? Match the words with the situations.

1 Wait a minute! One by one!

2 Stand on each other's shoulders down there!

3 I'm going to hit the clock.

4 You stole my invention!

5 Shaun, do something! Help!

6 Preston's going to make them into dog food.

a ☐ 4 Wallace says when he sees his *Knitting Machine*.

b ☐ Wallace says to the sheep following Shaun out of the lorry.

c ☐ thinks Gromit when he sees Preston's sign on the town clock.

d ☐ cries Wendolene when the tube of the dryer starts to suck Wallace into it.

e ☐ Wallace says to the sheep on the motorbike.

f ☐ thinks Gromit in his plane when he first sees the clock in the town square.

WORD WORK

1 Find words from Chapter 7 in the planes.

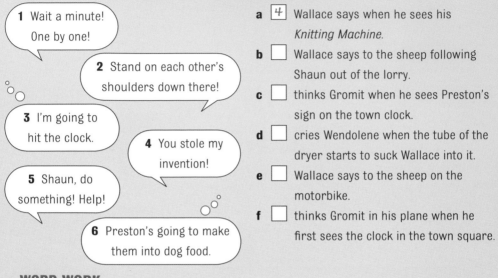

a l <u>ow</u>   W O L

b w _ _ _ _   ANGWO

c t _ _ _   EBUT

d w _ _ _ _ _   DONOWE

e b _ _ _ _ _   KCRIBS

f s _ _ _ _ _ _ _   WAISSDEY

g t _ _ _ _ _ _ _ _   WHORT YAAW

h t _ _ _ _ _ _   WTDOSAR

2 Complete the sentences with the words from Activity 1.

a Gromit flies his plane high up in the sky, and then ...... low .... down near the ground.

b That isn't a metal chair; it's a .... chair.

c Don't .... yesterday's newspaper. I want to read it.

d In my street-cleaning machine, soapy water comes out through a long ....

e He looked .... to see the famous film star who was sitting on his right at the next table in the restaurant.

f The thieves ran away when they saw a police car driving .... them.

g The train was pulling a .... full of stones.

h A lot of houses in Britain are made of red ....

GUESS WHAT

What happens in the next chapter? Tick the boxes.

a We learn that Preston . . .

1 ☐ is a robot.

2 ☐ is Wendolene's father in a dog suit.

3 ☐ is really a cat.

b . . . falls into the *Dog Food Machine*.

1 ☐ Gromit

2 ☐ Preston

3 ☐ Shaun

c Wendolene comes to see Wallace . . .

1 ☐ to thank him for mending Preston.

2 ☐ to ask him to marry her.

3 ☐ to tell him that she doesn't like cheese.

d In the end . . .

1 ☐ Wallace and Gromit are alone again.

2 ☐ Wendolene and Wallace get married.

3 ☐ Shaun stays with Wallace and Gromit.

Chapter 8

A happy ending

Inside the factory the side-car flew towards Preston. It was getting lower all the time. Gromit pushed a green button, and the porridge gun shot at Preston, and hit him again and again in the face. Gromit was still flying towards Preston, but at the last minute Preston put out his hands and caught the propeller of the plane. The propeller stopped moving but the plane started turning round and round very fast. Gromit flew out of his plane seat and went up into the air. He landed on a high **ledge** in the factory. At the same time Shaun took the end of the rope that went round the tube of the dryer and pulled it. As Shaun pulled the rope, the tube moved nearer to Preston. When the tube was above Preston it sucked him up into the *Knitting Machine*.

On the *Knitting Machine* the dial was on *Light Shave*. Gromit **swung** down from the ledge with a rope and turned the dial to **Close Shave**.

'Good lad,' said Wallace. 'Now Preston will learn not to be so bad!'

The clippers on the machine cut off all Preston's hair and made it into dog-hair wool. Then the machine knitted the dog-hair wool into a dog-hair pullover. While this was happening Preston started to hit the sides of the *Knitting Machine* from the inside.

'He's **malfunctioning**!' said Wendolene.

'Mal— what?' asked Wallace.

'Malfunctioning. Preston is a **cyber** dog,' said Wendolene.

'A cyber what?' asked Wallace.

'A **robot**,' explained Wendolene.

Suddenly Preston's robot arm hit the *Knitting Machine* very hard and made a hole in the side of it.

ledge a long flat thing that you can stand on high above the ground

swing (*past* **swung**) to move from left to right on the end of a rope

close shave when a man cuts the hair on his face very carefully; when you nearly have an accident but in the end are lucky and escape from danger

malfunction to go wrong, not to work well

cyber having something to do with computers

robot a machine that looks and moves like a person or animal

'Daddy invented him to keep me safe, but now he's evil,' went on Wendolene.

Preston's robot arm came out of the hole in the side of the machine, and opened the machine door. Then Preston walked out. There was no hair on him now – he was a terrible metal robot dog!

Preston walked nearer and nearer to Shaun and put out his arms to catch him. Suddenly Gromit swung down on his rope, caught Shaun in his hands, and swung back up to the safe ledge again. Preston's robot arms closed on nothing.

The evil robot dog turned angrily to Wallace and Wendolene. But, just then, the *Knitting Machine* put the dog-hair pullover over Preston's head. He couldn't see anything and he hit a lever by mistake. The lever moved the **platform** that Wallace, Wendolene, the sheep, and Preston were on, and it went up into the air. Now they were standing in front of a green **conveyor belt** that went to the *Dog Food Machine*.

'That's a clever machine,' Wallace said, when he saw the big metal teeth of the machine.

platform a flat thing that you stand on

conveyor belt a moving platform that takes things into, through, or away from a machine

There was a loud whistle from somewhere above them. It was Gromit. He swung down on his rope and knocked Preston off the platform and onto the conveyor belt. Then Gromit dropped from the rope and landed on the conveyor belt, too. The conveyor belt was moving towards the *Dog Food Machine*. Preston angrily pulled the dog-hair pullover into pieces so he could see again. When he saw the metal teeth of the *Dog Food Machine* in front of him, he started running away from them. By now Gromit was running, too. He was running away from the machine and from Preston.

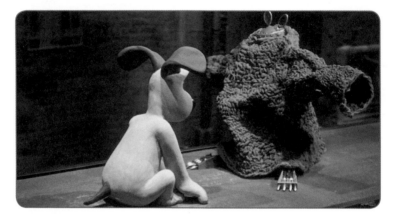

'Do something, Wallace!' cried Wendolene.

Wallace pressed a button – but it was the wrong one. The conveyor belt moved faster and Preston and Gromit had to run faster, too. Wallace pressed another button, but it was also the wrong one. This time the platform moved up, and Wallace, Wendolene, and the sheep all fell onto the conveyor belt. The conveyor belt took them nearer to the *Dog Food Machine*, but Wallace, Wendolene and the sheep ran away from it as fast as they could. Gromit and Preston were behind them. They were all running away from the machine, but the conveyor belt was carrying them all towards those terrible big metal teeth.

Shaun was still on the ledge above them. Quickly he tied a big heavy metal **weight** to the end of the rope. Then he swung down with the metal weight towards the conveyor belt.

Wendolene looked up and saw Shaun. 'Quick! Heads down!' she cried.

Wallace, Wendolene, the sheep, and Gromit quickly put their heads down. Shaun and the big weight flew over them, hit Preston, and pushed him into the mouth of the *Dog Food Machine*. The metal teeth closed on Preston and broke his metal body into a thousand pieces, and then the machine stopped working.

Wallace, Gromit and Wendolene were safe at last.

'We were nearly tins of dog food then,' said Wallace.

weight a heavy metal thing

Then they heard a strange noise from the *Dog Food Machine* and looked round. Another part of the machine was putting lots of little metal pieces into empty tins, which said *Preston's Dog Food*.

That was the end of Preston's robot body.

remote control
something without wires that you hold in your hand to make a machine work from far away

The next day, there was a ring at the front door of 62 West Wallaby Street.

Wallace opened the door, and saw Wendolene there.

'I couldn't walk past and not come to say thank you,' said Wendolene. 'Preston's a nice dog again, like he was before,' she said.

She touched a **remote control** in her hand, and the robot dog Preston arrived with a newspaper in his mouth. He gave it to Wallace.

'Thank you Preston,' said Wallace, and then he looked at Wendolene. 'Tell me if he goes wrong again.'

'That's very nice of you,' said Wendolene.

'Would you like to come in? We're going to have some cheese.'

'Oh, no. Not cheese. Sorry. It makes me ill. I really don't like it.'

Wallace suddenly felt very sad.

'We must go home now. Come on, Preston,' said Wendolene. And she pressed some buttons on the remote control. She walked out of the front garden with Preston. At the gate, she looked back at Wallace. 'Goodbye,' she said, and she waved. Then she walked away down the street.

Back in the front room, Wallace sat in his comfortable chair.

'What's wrong with cheese?' he said to himself sadly.

Gromit was reading the newspaper. The headline on the front page said:

GROMIT FREE!

'Speaking of cheese . . . ,' said Wallace, and he looked happier, 'there's going to be more of it for both of us. And no sheep to worry us.' Wallace laughed. He took the cover off the cheese **dish** hungrily, but there – under the cover – was Shaun the sheep, and he was busy eating Wallace's cheese.

'Get off my cheese!' cried Wallace. 'Gromit,' he called, 'Get him!'

But Gromit went on reading the newspaper. And Shaun went on eating Wallace's cheese.

'Baa, baa,' he cried happily.

dish a big plate

READING CHECK

Put these sentences in the correct order. Number them 1–8.

a ☐ The tube sucks Preston into the *Knitting Machine*.

b ☐ Gromit knocks Preston onto the conveyor belt.

c ☐ Preston comes out of the *Dog Food Machine* in little pieces.

d ☐ Gromit flies into the factory and shoots porridge at Preston.

e ☐ Wallace presses the wrong button and they all land on the conveyor belt.

f ☐ Preston gets out of the *Knitting Machine* and is a metal robot dog.

g ☐ Shaun swings over them and knocks Preston into the *Dog Food Machine*.

h ☐ Wendolene visits Wallace to thank him for mending Preston.

WORD WORK

Use the words in the metal weight to complete Wallace's diary on page 55.

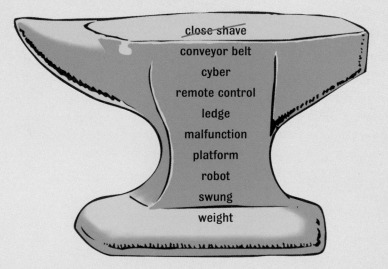

close shave
conveyor belt
cyber
remote control
ledge
malfunction
platform
robot
swung
weight

We had a (a) .....close..... .....shave..... in the dog food factory yesterday. We found out that Wendolene's dog, Preston, was really a metal (b) .... Preston started to (c) .... when he was in the Knitting Machine. After that Preston began to run after Gromit along the green (d) .... in front of the Dog Food Machine. I pushed the wrong button and Wendolene, all the sheep, and I fell off the (e) .... that we were standing on. Suddenly we all found ourselves moving towards the Dog Food Machine. But luckily Shaun was high up on a (f) .... and he (g) .... down on a rope to save us, and knocked Preston into the machine with a heavy metal (h) ....

Today Wendolene came to see me with Preston. I mended him after his accident. He is now a good (i) .... dog and Wendolene can control him by pressing the buttons on his (j) ....

GUESS WHAT

What happens in the next Wallace and Gromit story? Choose from these ideas or add your own.

a ☐ Wallace, Gromit, and Shaun go away on holiday together.

b ☐ Wallace and Gromit start growing vegetables.

c ☐ Wallace and Gromit start driving around in a car instead of on a motorbike.

d ☐ Wallace meets a woman from a rich family and forgets Gromit.

e ☐ Gromit has more fights with another bad dog.

f ☐ ....

g ☐ ....

PROJECT A *Invitation Letters*

1 Read the invitation letter and complete the table.

> 62 West Wallaby Street,
> Newton, NE1 4AT
>
> 29th October
>
> Dear Wendolene,
>
> I am writing to invite you to a cheese-tasting party at my house on the 6th November at 4 p.m. We are going to taste some Italian Cheese (Gorgonzola), English Cheese (Cheddar), and French Cheese (Camembert). If you don't like the cheese, you can eat the biscuits.
>
> I hope you can come. Please bring Preston. Gromit will be happy to see him.
>
> Yours,
>
> Wallace

Who is writing the letter?	
What's his/her address?	
What's the date of the letter?	
Who is the letter to?	
What kind of party is it an invitation to?	
Where is the party?	
When is the party?	
Who will be there?	
What are they going to do?	

2 Does Wendolene accept or refuse Wallace's invitation? Rewrite her reply using the correct punctuation and the correct layout on the page.

> Wendolene's Wool Shop The Town Square Newton IM4 T42 30th October Dear Wallace Thank you for your kind invitation I'm sorry but I'm afraid I can't come to the cheese-tasting party at your house on the 6th November at 4pm Preston needs to go to the robot factory and you know that I don't like cheese Preston sends his best wishes Yours Wendolene

3 Use the information in the table to write an invitation letter from Wendolene. Use the letter in Activity 1 to help you.

Who is writing the letter?	Wendolene
What's his/her address?	Wendolene's Wool Shop, The Town Square, Newton, IM4 T42
What's the date of the letter?	15th November
Who is the letter to?	Wallace
What kind of party is it an invitation to?	a knitting party
Where is the party?	at Wendolene's shop
When is the party?	6th December at 3 p.m.
Who will be there?	Wendolene and Preston
What are they going to do?	Knit pullovers with English, Australian, and New Zealand wool

4 Write Wallace's reply, either accepting or refusing the invitation.

PROJECT B   *Inventions*

1 Match the inventions with the inventors.

a Karl Benz

b Alexander Graham Bell

1 telephone

2 electric light

c Guglielmo Marconi

d John Logie Baird

3 car

4 radio

e Thomas Alva Edison

f Wilbur and Orville Wright

5 aeroplane

6 television

2 Read the essay. Is the writer for or against television? Do you agree?

Are you _for_ or _against_ television? Why?

Many people are against television, but I think it's a good thing.

Some people say that we watch too much television. Today a lot of young people are fat and unhealthy because they spend too much time in front of the television. In addition, some programmes are not good for young people to watch because there's a lot of fighting, murders, and bad language.

I don't agree. I think that television is a good thing. We can see the news while it is happening. We can get a lot of information and there are educational programmes, too. In addition, television can make information about the past – or life in other countries – more interesting and easier to understand than books.

So some people think that television is a bad thing. But I feel that television is a good way of getting information.

3 Read the essay again. Complete the table.

Invention	
Writer's opinion: for or against	
What are the arguments against?	●
	●
	●
What are the arguments for?	●
	●
	●
Writer's conclusion	

4 **Here are some more modern inventions. Choose one and complete the table with notes about it.**

mobile phone   MP3 player   computer game

satellite TV   skateboard   the Internet

Invention	
Your opinion: for or against	
What are the arguments against?	● ● ●
What are the arguments for?	● ● ●
Your conclusion	

Remember
If you are 'for' the invention, put the arguments 'against' first.
If you are 'against' the invention, put the arguments 'for' first.

5 **Use your notes from Activity 4 and write an essay about your invention. Use the essay in Activity 2 to help you.**

GRAMMAR CHECK

Past Simple and Past Continuous

We use the Past Simple to describe finished events in the past.

We use the Past Continuous to talk about a longer activity that began before and was in progress when the events in the Past Simple occurred. We use was/were with the present participle.

When Wallace first saw Wendolene, she was knitting.
             (Past Simple)   (Past Continuous)

1 Answer the questions about the beginning of the story. Use the words in brackets.

   a What was Gromit doing at the beginning of the story? (knit) .He. was. knitting..

   b What was Wallace doing? (sleep) ....

   c What did Gromit hear? (hear / noise) ....

   d Where did the lorry stop? (stop / red light) ....

   e What did the small sheep do? (escape / lorry) ....

   f What was Gromit doing later that morning? (sit / kitchen) ....

   g What did Wallace have for breakfast? (have / porridge) ....

   h How did Wallace and Gromit go to the wool shop? (go / motorbike) ....

2 Complete the text about Wallace and Wendolene using the Past Simple or the Past Continuous.

While Gromit a) .was. cleaning. (clean) the windows, Wallace b) .... (look) into the shop. Inside the shop there c) .... (be) a woman with short brown hair and dark eyes. She d) .... (knit). She e) .... (look up) and f) .... (see) Wallace. Then she g) .... (put down) her knitting and she h) .... (smile) at him. Wallace i) .... (walk) into the shop. A guard dog j) ....(read) a newspaper in the corner. He k) .... (not smile) when he saw Wallace.

GRAMMAR CHECK

Direct and reported speech

In direct speech we give the words that people say or think.	In reported speech we put the verb one step into the past, and change the pronouns and the possessive adjectives.
'I'm going to crash!' thought Gromit.	*Gromit thought that he was going to crash.*
'Oooh! I can't go any faster!' cried Wallace.	*Wallace cried that he couldn't go any faster.*

When we report questions we change the order of the pronoun and verb.

'What are you doing, Preston?' asked Wendolene.	*Wendolene asked Preston what he was doing.*

3 Rewrite direct speech as reported speech.

a 'Preston is my guard dog,' explained Wendolene.

Wendolene explained that Preston was her guard dog.

b 'The windows are very clean,' she said.

....

c 'Shaun is going to have a wash,' explained Wallace.

....

d 'Why are you eating everything, Shaun?' asked Gromit.

....

e 'I invent things,' Wallace told Wendolene.

....

f 'Preston is a horrible dog,' thought Gromit.

....

g 'Where are you going, Shaun?' asked Wallace.

....

h 'We don't want to be dog meat!' cried all the sheep.

....

....

Verb + infinitive or –ing form

After the verbs *begin, forget, learn, like, need, remember, want, ask, tell, try, decide*, and *would like* we use to + infinitive.

Gromit decided to help the sheep.

After the verbs *begin, finish, go, like, love, stop, enjoy, prefer*, and *go on* we use verb + –ing.

Wallace went on working.

4 **Complete these sentences about the story with the *to* + infinitive or verb + *–ing* form of the verb in brackets.**

   a Wallace told Shaun .to.stop. (stop) eating the newspaper.

   b All the sheep wanted .... (read) the newspaper.

   c Gromit didn't enjoy .... (be) in prison.

   d Wallace needed .... (make) a ladder for Gromit.

   e Wallace was uncomfortable but he went on .... (hold up) the sheep.

   f Poor Shaun couldn't stop .... (shake).

   g Preston began .... (growl) at Shaun.

   h Preston tried................... (drive) the lorry faster and faster.

   i Gromit remembered .... (push) the buttons at the front of the side-car.

   j Wendolene asked Wallace .... (rescue) her.

   k Wallace went .... (help) Wendolene.

   l Wallace would like .... (marry) Wendolene.

GRAMMAR CHECK

Prepositions of movement

Prepositions of movement tell us how something moves.

up	down	into
out of	over	through
across	past	to

5 Complete the text with the prepositions in the box.

across	down	~~into~~	into	out of
over	past	through	to	up

Preston climbed a) ....into........ the driver's seat and started the lorry. He drove the lorry out of the field and onto the road. While Preston was driving down the dark road, Gromit jumped b) .... the side-car. He drove c) .... an old garage but he couldn't see the lorry. Suddenly, the lorry came d) .... the garage. Now it was behind Gromit! Gromit had an idea. He put the ladder in front of Wallace. Then he climbed e) .... to the top of the ladder and caught some telephone wires in his hands. The motorbike went up in the air and came f) .... again behind the lorry. But they weren't safe. The side-car broke away from the motorbike. The motorbike followed the road but the side-car went g) .... the road from one side to the other and hit a sign.

Wallace was driving fast behind the lorry now. He opened the door of the lorry. His feet were on the ladder and his body was making a bridge across the road between the ladder and the lorry. He looked h) .... the open door and he saw Shaun the sheep. Shaun walked up i) .... the door of the lorry. Then he walked j) .... Wallace's back and along the ladder. The sheep then followed one by one over the 'bridge'.

GRAMMAR CHECK

Modal auxiliary verbs: can, could, must, and have to

There are different modal forms and meanings. We use can/could to express ability, permission, or requests. After can/could, we use infinitive without *to*.

Gromit couldn't drive faster.   *I can speak French.* (ability)

Each person can buy only two balls of wool. (permission)

Can/Could I ask you a question? (request)

We use must (not) to express strong obligation or prohibition. After must, we use infinitive without *to*.

I must go and investigate. (strong obligation)

You mustn't smoke on the aeroplane. (prohibition)

We use have to/don't have to to say that something is necessary or not necessary.

You don't have to answer me now.   *I have to go to bed because I'm very tired.*

6 **Choose the correct word to complete the sentences.**

   a Wallace wanted to go faster but he (couldn't)/can't.

   b Wallace said, 'You **must/have** leave the country, Gromit. The police are looking for you.'

   c 'We have/Can to rescue the sheep,' said Gromit

   d 'You **don't have/mustn't** to eat the cheesc, Wendolene,' said Wallace sadly.

   e 'I **mustn't/couldn't** walk past and not say thank you,' said Wendolene.

   f 'Could/Have I look at the newspaper?' asked Shaun.

7 **Complete the text about Wendolene with suitable modal forms.**

Wendolene a) ..could.. not leave Preston becausc he was a present from her father. She b) .... to look after him. But she knew that Preston was bad. 'Preston c) .... be good: he makes sheep into dog meat!', she cried, 'I d) .... ask for help – but who e) .... help me?' When Wendolene met Wallace, she liked him but she f) .... be open with him. Wallace knew there was something wrong. 'I g) .... help this woman,' he thought. He didn't say anything to Gromit about Wendolene. He just said, 'Come on, Gromit. We h) .... clean these windows now. It's late!'

GRAMMAR CHECK

Question tags

We use question tags to check information, or to ask someone to agree with us.
The tag contains subject + main verb or auxiliary verb to match the sentence.

If the sentence is affirmative, the question tag is negative.

You can knit, can't you?

If the sentence is negative, the question tag is affirmative.

You can't invent things, can you?

With most tenses, we repeat the main verb or auxiliary verb in the question tag.

He's a nice boy, isn't he?

They haven't bought a dog, have they?

You do like him, don't you?

He isn't driving, is he?

They aren't going to kill him, are they?

I didn't leave the door open, did I?

She was eating my cheese, wasn't she?

We won't be late, will we?

8 What did Wallace say to Gromit? Complete the sentences with question tags.

  a You need some wool, <u>don't you?</u>

  b You'll have porridge for breakfast, ...?

  c You aren't still sleeping, ...?

  d We must go to the High Street, ...?

  e We don't need to take the motorbike,

      ....?

  f You've got everything, ...?

9 What did Wallace say to Wendolene? Complete the sentences with the correct auxiliary verb (or main verb) and a question tag.

  a You / not love me, ...? <u>You don't love me, do you?</u>

  b We / having / nice time, ...? ....

  c He is / clever dog, ...? ....

  d You / running / away, ...? ....

  e You / not bought / any wool recently, ...? ....

  f You / not going / eat the cheese, ...? ....